North York Moors National Park

''a marvellous freedom from
the tumult of the world''

(St. Ailred of Rievaulx Abbey, 1143)

Foreword

In 1952, the North York Moors was designated by Parliament as a National Park — one of 10 such Parks in England and Wales. The scenery of this corner of Yorkshire richly deserves such a title. The beauty of its moorland, dale and coastal landscapes is a heritage we greatly cherish and must jealously guard. The law of the land places very clear duties upon the National Park Committee to protect the beauty of the landscape, to promote the enjoyment of visitors and to support the interests of those who live and work in the Park.

It is important to remember that despite the word 'National' the land is privately owned and is a place of work for farmers, gamekeepers and foresters. We ask all our visitors to observe decent countryside manners and to give no one cause to regret their visit.

Martin Hewitt

(Chairman, North York Moors National Park Committee)

ACKNOWLEDGEMENTS

Photos: Ian Carstairs — cover photo, 3, 6, 11, 13, 17, 18 bottom, 20, 21 bottom, 22 bottom, 23, 26 right, 29, 30, 35 bottom, 36; Yorkshire and Humberside Tourist Board 14, 15, 28 left; Alex Marwood 10, 35 top; Mike Herringshaw 24; Roy A. Harris and K.R. Duff 33 top left; Frank Broadbent 33 bottom left.
Text: Ian P. Sampson — National Park Information Service
Design: Julie A. Gow — National Park Information Service.

ISBN 0907480 00 4   *AB PRINTERS LTD, LEICESTER (0533) 769921*

The Moors Centre, Danby

Contents

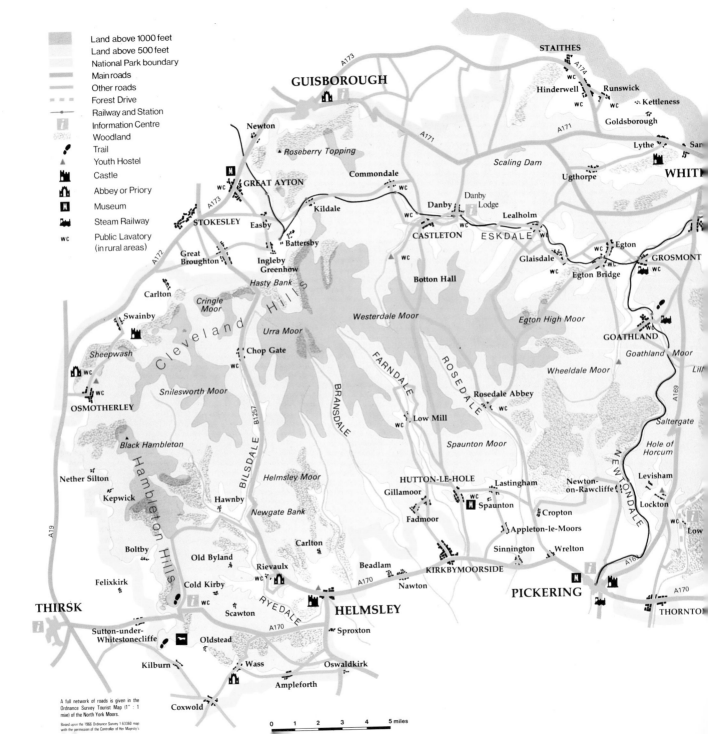

Legend

- Land above 1000 feet
- Land above 500 feet
- National Park boundary
- Main roads
- Other roads
- Forest Drive
- Railway and Station
- Information Centre
- Woodland
- Trail
- Youth Hostel
- Castle
- Abbey or Priory
- Museum
- Steam Railway
- Public Lavatory (in rural areas)

GUISBOROUGH

STAITHES
A174
Hinderwell
Runswick
Kettleness
Goldsborough
Lythe
Sar
WHIT

A173
Newton
Roseberry Topping
Commondale
Scaling Dam
Ugthorpe
A171

GREAT AYTON
Kildale
Danby
Danby Lodge
Lealholm
STOKESLEY
Easby
CASTLETON
ESKDALE
Egton
Glaisdale
GROSMONT
Battersby
Egton Bridge
Great Broughton
Ingleby Greenhow
Botton Hall

Hasty Bank
Carlton
Cringle Moor
Westerdale Moor
Egton High Moor
Swainby
GOATHLAND
Goathland Moor
Lill
Sheepwash
Urra Moor
Chop Gate
Wheeldale Moor
Snilesworth Moor
FARNDALE
ROSEDALE
Rosedale Abbey
Saltergate
OSMOTHERLEY
BRANSDALE
Low Mill
Spaunton Moor
Hole of Horcum
Black Hambleton
Helmsley Moor
HUTTON-LE-HOLE
Lastingham
Newton-on-Rawcliffe
Levisham
Nether Silton
Gillamoor
Spaunton
Lockton
Kepwick
Hawnby
Newgate Bank
Fadmoor
Cropton
Appleton-le-Moors
Low
Boltby
Carlton
Sinnington
Wrelton
Old Byland
Rievaulx
Beadlam
KIRKBYMOORSIDE
Felixkirk
Cold Kirby
Nawton
A170
PICKERING
THIRSK
Scawton
HELMSLEY
THORNTO
Sutton-under-Whitestonecliffe
Oldstead
Sproxton
A170
Kilburn
Wass
Oswaldkirk
Ampleforth
Coxwold

A172
A19
B1257
BILSDALE
Hambleton Hills
Cleveland Hills
RYEDALE
NEWTONDALE
A169
A170

A full network of roads is given in the
Ordnance Survey Tourist Map (1" : 1
mile) of the North York Moors.

Based upon the 1966 Ordnance Survey 1:63360 map
with the permission of the Controller of Her Majesty's

0 1 2 3 4 5 miles

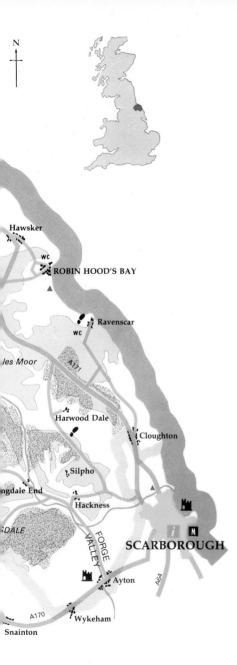

Introduction

Tucked away in a corner of north-east England is an isolated upland block of open countryside — a series of high moors and narrow intervening dales known collectively as the **North York Moors**. Set hard up against a rocky North Sea coast, the Moors appear to stand aloof from all that goes on in the horseshoe area of the surrounding lowland plains. It was this **remoteness** which made these moors one of the last outposts of a self-sufficient way of life which once typified the rural areas of England. By today's standard of tourism, it still remains relatively 'undiscovered'.

This **collection of moorlands and dales** was anciently known as 'Blackamor'; by 1890 it was known in Bulmer's History & Directory of North Yorkshire 'by the general name of North York Moors'. Here is a range of scenery from high, wild moorlands to quiet pastoral dales and bordered on the east by an **impressive rugged coastline**. It contains some of the finest landscapes in the country and in 1952 was officially designated as one of the ten National Parks in England and Wales.

The **title** 'National Park' is a bit misleading — it does not mean that the Park is owned by the nation! In fact the land is owned mainly by those who live and work there — the farmers, foresters and other private landowners. Over 80% of the Park is in **private ownership** and it is just as private as anyone else's farmland. The word 'National' is used not in the sense of 'ownership' but in the sense of 'being in the interest of the nation'. On behalf of us all, an Act of Parliament has put its seal on the protection of this beautiful landscape and our enjoyment of it. Yes, there is a **warm welcome to visitors** — provided they follow the Country Code; yes, there is access to the farmland, moorland and dale — provided you follow the public rights of way. Within the North York Moors National Park there are over **1000 miles** of public footpaths and bridleways as well as many miles of green lanes and country roads.

Of all the scenic variety in the North York Moors, its distinctive character lies in the strength and beauty of its moors. No vision of Yorkshire would ever be complete without the **freedom, wildness and romance** of its moors but that is something you will have to discover for yourself.

The North York Moors

The name is appropriate, it tells you what it is — **moorland**, a seemingly boundless tract of heather clad upland, stretching across the central part of the Park. At Ralph Cross, on the Castleton to

Hutton-le-Hole road, you stand astride the main watershed running from west to east across the moorland. Few roads cross the watershed for the elevated ridge acts as a physical barrier isolating north from south. To the north the waters descend through small, deeply indented dales into the **River Esk**; to the south a series of larger dales carry the waters off the moors into the **River Derwent** system. It is these numerous dales which break up the landscape creating a pattern of alternate 'moor' and 'dale'. This is the distinctive character of the North York Moors, a collection of open heather moors, each with their own name, separated by a softer scene of picturesque dales.

The network of roads is a challenge of exploration to the visitor — the intricacies of the Esk Valley routes need more attention to the roadmap than most. Each dale is a new discovery and offers something of its own individual charm and character. The narrower valleys are often avoided by the moorland roads which keep to the 'riggs' or ridges, sometimes cutting clean across the moor. These provide the motorist with an immense **panorama of moor and dale.**

The Park is a compact area, more easily defined by its physical boundaries than most. To the east is 25 miles of North Sea coastline, to the south the Vale of Pickering, to the west the Vales of York and Mowbray extending northwards to the flat lands of the Cleveland Plain and Teesside. Within its 553 square miles (1432 square kilometres) the National Park possesses a **variety of scenery** far greater than one might at first appreciate — wild moors, pastoral dales, extensive forests, steep escarpments, coastal cliffs and rich agricultural lands along the southern edge.

The scenery of the coastline is one of **dramatic cliffs**, rarely less than 200 feet and reaching almost 700 feet at Boulby Cliff. Within the National Park boundary, which excludes

Scarborough, Whitby and Sandsend, there are 25 miles of very beautiful and unspoilt coastline — one of the prime duties of the National Park authority is to see that it **remains unspoilt**. With such a cliffed coastline it is not surprising to find

The patchwork pattern of fields in Little Fryup Dale. The tree line in the dale bottom marks the course of Little Fryup Beck as it flows north-eastwards to join the River Esk.
Overleaf: Farndale

only 3 villages with direct access to the sea — **Staithes, Runswick** and **Robin Hood's Bay**. These picturesque villages sit tight on the edge of the land, their close-packed houses perched almost on top of one another on the steep access to the sea. Each has its one main street down to the beach with a maze of cobbled 'ginnels' or passageways between the houses. The atmosphere is one of intimacy and the scene belongs to the days of the smugglers who passed the contraband along the alleyways and even from house to house under the nose of the customs men.

The North Sea continues a merciless onslaught along this coast wearing it away at an average rate of 3 inches each year and up to 3 feet or more in some locations. Past generations have seen many of the sea-front cottages washed away by raging seas and in 1682 the whole village of Runswick fell captive to the sea. Today, coastal protection measures such as the sea wall at Robin Hood's Bay are designed to preserve these village gems.

A well-known landmark in the North York Moors is the giant turf-cut figure of the **'White Horse'** above the village of Kilburn on the south-western edge of the Park. There is a clue here to the local geology for turf-cut figures are found where the rocks are either chalk or limestone. In fact we 'cheat' a little. The rock is **limestone** but the 'Horse' does get the occasional grooming of chalk chippings to keep it 'White'. It is this outcrop of limestone stretching across the southern fringe of the Park which provides a sweeping contrast in scenery and land-use to the central moorlands. The rich brown earths of the limestone provide the most fertile land in the National Park. The **Hambleton Hills** run south from Osmotherley down to Sutton Bank and around to Helmsley at

a height of up to 1000 feet above sea level. The **steep western escarpment** provides a well-defined physical boundary and a line of vantage points, such as at Sutton Bank, from which to gaze across 20 miles of vale to the Pennine Dales.

Between Helmsley and Scarborough the land rises gently northwards out of the Vale of Pickering and flattens out to form a relatively narrow belt of limestone hills some 2 to 3 miles wide. They are known as the **Tabular Hills** because they appear as 'flat as a table'. These hills come to a sudden and abrupt end in a steep north-facing escarpment edge. This 'break' in the landscape forms one of the most impressive scenic features in the moors (e.g. Saltergate Bank on the Pickering to Whitby road) and can be traced for some 25 miles right along the northern edge of the Tabular Hills from Rievaulx Moor to Silpho Moor. The break is so sudden that there are a number of **surprise views** which await the unsuspecting motorist travelling northwards into the moors. A panorama of moorland and dale comes suddenly into view as at 'Surprise View', Gillamoor. The waters of the Rye, Riccal, Hodge, Dove, Seven, Pickering Beck and River Derwent all drain southwards from the moorland watershed and cut deep narrow valleys through the limestone escarpment. The resulting tabular blocks stand as **silent sentries**, almost sphinx-like, guarding the access from the central moorland.

The rolling **Cleveland Hills** complete the western defences of the Park, extending northwards from Osmotherley. Amongst these heather-topped hills we find the **highest point** in the moors at Botton Head (1489 feet) on Urra Moor. These hills have been subjected to man's industrial exploitation in the past and although the evidence of jet, alum and ironstone mines are there to be seen, they detract little from the overall boldness and wildness of the landscape.

Signs of the Past

Who were the original British or English people? Our **ancestoral lines** reach back, through a tangle of invading armies, to Stone Age times. Stone Age man crossed from the continent and others followed from various parts of Europe. And so they came, through the Bronze and Iron Ages to the Romans, Angles, Saxons, Danes, Vikings and Normans. The North York Moors has played host to all these ancestors. We are interested here in the things which they left behind, the remains which we can see today and in the story they tell us of life in the past.

The earliest signs of pre-historic man which have survived some 5000 years of time are his **burial grounds**. A glance at the 1″ to 1 mile Ordnance Survey Tourist Map of the Park will reveal the repeated appearance of the words 'tumuli', 'tumulus', 'howes' and 'howe' on the high moors. These are burial mounds or barrows and in the North York Moors the larger barrows have come to be known as **howes** — from the Scandinavian name for a burial mound 'haugr'.

Apart from a few communal burial mounds of the New Stone Age (3000-1800 B.C.), the vast number of tumuli and howes were built by the **Bronze Age** people (1800-500 B.C.) who spread across the moors. The Park is studded with these barrows which vary from slight bumps in the heather to imposing mounds up to 20 feet high and 100 feet in diameter. There are over 3000 of these howes and many of them have **individual names**, e.g. Loose Howe, Lilla Howe, Pick Howe, etc. The surprising thing is to find that these people settled right across the inhospitable high moors. However, investigations have shown that the climate was warmer and drier than it is today and 'home' was probably some tent or wooden shelter of which time has destroyed all trace.

Ralph Cross — chosen as the emblem of the North York Moors National Park. An imposing stone cross, nine feet tall, standing in the almost geographical centre of the moors.

Opposite: Wade's Causeway. A preserved stretch of Roman road, built almost 2,000 years ago, cuts across Wheeldale Moor.

On the edge of **Wheeldale Moor**, 600 feet above sea level, is a 1¼ mile stretch of preserved road. Hundreds of people walk along it each year following in the footsteps of the first Roman soldiers to reach these northern moors.

11

The **Romans** had begun their conquest of England in 43 A.D. and reached Yorkshire around 70 A.D. One of the reasons for the great success of Roman occupation was their road building programme and the road across the moors was just one of a communication system radiating out from the legionary fortress at Malton. The road probably reached over the moorlands to the coast but its coastal terminus has never been discovered. Locally the road is called **Wade's Causeway** after the giant who, legend has it, built the road for the convenience of his wife as she walked across the moors to take their cattle to market.

If we are to single out one item of unique interest to the Park, it must be the **stone moorland cross**. No other area can boast of such a concentration for there are over 30 named moorland crosses in the North York Moors. **Lilla Cross**, standing in splendid solitude on Fylingdales Moor, is thought to be the oldest Christian monument in Northern England. It commemorates the death of Lilla who, in 626, used himself to shield King Edwin from an assassin's dagger — a brave action which cost Lilla his own life. Most of the crosses however have less heroic origins and were set up in medieval time as **waymarkers** to guide travellers across the desolate moors. In recognition of the importance of these crosses the National Park Committee chose **Ralph Cross** which stands near the head of Rosedale, as the **emblem** for this National Park.

At **Lastingham** we stand on ground first hallowed by St. Cedd in the pioneer days of Christian mission work in the 7th century. What we come to see, however, dates from the 11th century and lies underground below the present church. Here is one of the finest examples of a **crypt** or underground burial chapel. The massive columns and vaulted roof have withstood the last 900 years

and are an impressive tribute to the achievements of Norman architecture. We owe Lastingham's crypt to the efforts of St. Stephen during his 10 year (1078-1088) stay here before being driven out by thieves and marauders. An interesting booklet, in the church, records the detail of its history.

One of the most glorious settings for a church is that in Kirkdale of **St. Gregory's Minster**, between Helmsley and Kirkbymoorside. Its story begins in the 7th century as a small mission church but 200 years later it was pillaged and destroyed by the ruthless Danes. It remained broken and fallen for another 200 years before being re-built around 1060 by Orm Gamalson, a wealthy Northumbrian overlord. A glance over the main door of the little church will reveal its most famous relic — a **Saxon sundial**. This is the rarest sundial in England. It bears the longest inscription known of the Anglo-Saxon period and with a little patience you will be able to decipher the Northumbrian English.

The **castles** and **abbeys** which we see today are a reminder of the last successful military invasion of this country. It was William the Conqueror and his Norman barons who not only introduced the building of castles into England but also invited groups of monks to come over from France and establish their abbeys and monasteries.

The earliest castles of the 11th century were built of timber on a raised mound or 'motte'. By the **12th century** they were being built of stone and if you go 'castle hunting' today you will most likely visit the ruins of Helmsley, Pickering and Scarborough — all dating back some 800 years. These are the monuments to medieval warfare and for 500 years they served not only as a military base but also as the centre of social and domestic life. Between 1100 and 1400 **Pickering**

A paved track near Commondale. The moors are crossed by a considerable number of tracks paved with flag-stones and known as trods, causeways or pannierman's tracks. These trods, just wide enough for one animal, were laid down to allow pack ponies to be dry-shod as

they carried their burden of goods across the moorland. The earliest trods, probably dating back to the 13th century, were built by the monastic institutions to transport goods from their vast and scattered estates.

Castle was visited by most English Kings for the hunting of deer and boar. The Forest of Pickering was a vast royal hunting ground stretching from Rosedale to the coast and as far north as the River Esk. Each castle has its own plan and history and you can explore these ruined strongholds with the aid of the booklets published by the Department of the Environment under whose care the buildings now come.

As well as the open air 'museum' of the countryside itself, an understanding of the past is aided by the collections to be seen in the **museums** around the Park. The museums of Scarborough, Whitby and Pickering have varied archaeological, historical and folk collections. The Ryedale Folk Museum in Hutton-le-Hole can boast of an exciting collection of items and reconstructed buildings of the district.

A Quiet Life

Those who walk the footpath from Helmsley to Rievaulx (3 miles) will find their first view of Ryedale from the top of Whinney Bank a generous reward. Perhaps the small band of monks who arrived to establish **Rievaulx Abbey** walked along this same route 800 years ago. The view would be different then — the forest cover would be extensive. The forest was the haunt of wolves and if the group of thirteen monks were wise they would have planned to reach their destination before dark. They had been given some land at Rievaulx by Walter l'Espec, Lord of Helmsley for the site of a new monastery.

Looking at the ruined remains of Rievaulx Abbey we can appreciate the success of those early Cistercian monks who laid the foundation in 1131 of the largest and finest Cistercian house in England. Even in its ruined state, the abbey reflects the skill which the stone masons had 800 years ago and also the wealth with which to finance such a magnificent building. The monasteries became rich partly through the donations received from the Norman gentry but even more so through their success as **sheep farmers**. Rievaulx Abbey had at one time more than 14,000 sheep on the moors around Ryedale and Bilsdale and the monks made a very successful business selling the wool to the cloth merchants who came over each year from Flanders, France and Italy.

For a hundred years the abbey thrived and under the third abbott, St. Ailred, there are said to have been 140 monks and over 500 lay brothers. One of the monks at Rievaulx, Walter Daniel, wrote that on feast days the church 'swarmed with them like a hive with bees'. Nowadays, on a warm summer weekend, Rievaulx 'swarms' not with monks but with visitors.

The valley floor at Rievaulx is quite narrow and to build the foundations for a large church they had to set it almost north to south. The one hundred and seventy foot long nave is impressive and it must have had an even greater impact on those who viewed it **800 years ago.**

The grandeur of the buildings was not reflected in the life of the monks, for these were men who lived with the barest of necessities. As long as basic needs were satisfied, the spiritual side of life was compensation enough. St. Ailred wrote of a 'marvellous freedom from the tumult of the world' and who has not dreamt of 'opting out' from the stresses and strains of everyday life?

The end of Rievaulx and all other monasteries came in the 16th century. Henry VIII ordered the closure of all the abbeys and monasteries throughout the country in his 'Dissolution of the Monasteries' in **1536**. His arguments with Rome and his envy of the monastic wealth led to his disapproval of all monastic institutions. After a life of 400 years Rievaulx Abbey was stripped of its treasures and useful building materials and some of the stone found its way into the construction of cottages in the village.

Rievaulx Abbey is considered by many to be the most beautiful in England.

Moorland Stone

Anyone who travels along the A170 from Sutton Bank to Scarborough, can hardly fail to notice the dominant colour of the stone used in building the village houses and field boundaries. The **stone walls** throughout the moors, are an indicator of the geology. As the stone changes from shades of grey to shades of brown we move from limestone to sandstone — the two most dominant rocks in the North York Moors.

The North York Moors has a **long history of mining and quarrying**. In times past, men have mined and quarried these moors for limestone, sandstone, ironstone, whinstone, coal, alum and jet. Some of these can be rightly claimed to be exclusive to the North York Moors!

The grey white stone which we see along the southern edge of the Park has been quarried from the belt of **limestone** which forms the Hambleton and Tabular Hills. In the south-west area, around Helmsley, the buildings often reveal a honey-coloured stone. The limestone here contains a greater proportion of sand and iron than elsewhere in the Park, resulting in a rich warm hue. Around nearly every village in the limestone belt you can find a number of small disused quarries. Not only was the stone used to build the farmhouses, it was also crushed and burnt to produce lime as an agricultural fertilizer for use locally and throughout the moors. Many of the farms in fact had their own **lime burning kiln** and a number of ruined kilns can still be found. The quarrying of the limestone today is confined to a few large quarries.

The massive **sandstone** rocks which form the heartland of the moors are responsible for giving the area its distinctive character — an expanse of gently rolling moorland and poor acid soils clothed with heather. These rocks provided a convenient source of **building stone** and the older houses and farmsteads have the distinctly warm colour of these yellowish, buff or brown sandstones. The capital city owes some of its buildings to North York Moors sandstone shipped out from Whitby harbour. A mile of quarries alongside the Aislaby to Egton road provided some of the sandstone to build the former London Bridge (now in America), the former Covent Garden Market, the Houses of Parliament, numerous seaside piers in this country and some in Europe.

Although all mining for ironstone has now ceased in the area, the local **ironstone** beds proved to be one of the richest sources of bedded iron ore in England. The pyramids of iron shale waste are particularly in evidence in the Cleveland area north of the Park boundary. The southern-most part of the ore field was in **Rosedale** where you can see the ruined remains of various buildings, roasting kilns and the track beds of the railway lines either side of the valley.

Whinstone is a local name given to the only igneous or volcanic rock in the Park. It originated as hot molten lava filling a crack in the earth's surface stretching 30 miles across the moors from Great Ayton almost to Ravenscar. It was extensively quarried and mined during the first half of this century to provide a crushed stone for **road making**.

The remains of plant life have formed thin but widespread deposits of poor quality **coal** in the moors. Despite its quality the coal was suitable for burning lime and in the 18th and 19th centuries excavations were widespread. Today there

The kilns at Rosedale Bank Top are a reminder of the days when the peace and tranquility of Rosedale were shattered by ironstone mining. The overcrowding of mineworkers in the village during the 1870's was *so severe that 'the beds were never cold' as shift replaced shift. The kilns were built for calcining or 'roasting' the ironstone to drive off water and gas, thereby reducing the weight of the transported ironstone.*

remains the depressions and waste tips of shaft workings and bell pits as above Rosedale Head to the east of Ralph Cross.

The **Alum** Shale is one of the rocks exclusive to the North York Moors. A cursory glance at the quarries and **shale tips** to be seen, for example at Sandsend, gives some idea of the scale of operation of this industry. Alum was in demand in the cloth industry as a mordant (fixer) of colour dyes and in the tanning of leather. There were over 20 alum quarries in the moors where the 100 foot thick alum shales outcropped and which were variously worked over a period of nearly 300 years (1600-1880).

'Whitby' jet is the second rock unique to this area. **Jet** is really fossilized drift wood from a coniferous tree somewhat akin to the present-day Monkey Puzzle tree. The black stone has been carved and polished to make jewellery and ornaments since ancient times. During the Victorian era, jet jewellery became the height of fashion and in the 1870s some 200 jet workshops in Whitby were busy meeting the demand. Miners had a tedious search in looking for deposits of this **semi-precious stone**. You can see their efforts marked by a string of spoil tips along the 900 foot contour line in the dale sides of the Cleveland Hills, e.g. south of the road over from Chop Gate, Bilsdale to Carlton-in-Cleveland.

17

Farming

The pace of change in the countryside has quickened in the last few decades and has been just as dramatic in some respects as change in the towns. Farm machinery grows in size and complexity, steel or timber framed asbestos buildings stand alongside the stone and pantile barns and steel silos can tower as high as the steeple of a village church. Despite the way in which technology and economic pressures have produced changes in farming practice, change has not been so dramatic in our moorland dales as in the lowland landscapes of the countryside.

Above: Mixed breeds of cattle used for beef production on a daleside farm.

Opposite: Sheep sale time at Fadmoor. A business and social occasion in the farming calendar.

There is a considerable variety in the type of farming amongst the 1300 or so farms in the North York Moors but **livestock farming** (rearing, fattening and dairying) is the major activity. The dale farms are a vital source of what are called 'store' lambs and cattle. Store means growing but not yet fattened and the moorland dales are the breeding ground for stock which will be sold off for fattening or for cross-breeding on the lower farms.

The monks of Rievaulx were the first large-scale sheep farmers in the North York Moors and the moors have continued to be used for **sheep grazing**. Today there are about 50,000 sheep on some 125,000 acres of moor. The hardy **Swaledale** breed is the most popular hill sheep for the open moorland. It is an easy breed to recognise with a black face, speckled grey nose and legs. The ewe has single curved horns and the ram has triple curved horns. The sheep live out on the moor for most of the year but will be brought into enclosed lower land for a few weeks during the lambing season. The rights to graze sheep on the moor are a very valuable possession to the dale farms, many of which will have less than 100 acres of improved land in the dale. Despite the trend to amalgamate and make bigger farms, a dale farm with a good moor stray is still a viable family farm.

Coming down off the moor top, the upper slopes of a dale provide rough pasture with the bottom lands put to grass and perhaps some cereals or root crops depending upon the soil conditions and other factors. **Grass** is the predominant feature of the farmed landscape in the North York Moors with about a quarter of the farmland being used for arable cultivation. When winter comes and the grass stops growing, the cattle and sheep have to be fed with alternative winter feedstuffs. Whether a farmer sells the young lambs and store cattle or keeps them for fattening will usually depend on the amount of land available for producing winter feed (hay or silage, barley, oats, roots). Some family run farms have turned to **dairy farming** and the bulk milk tankers are a common enough sight on the daleside roads.

Farming is the **major activity** in the North York Moors and approximately 2,300 people earn their living from farming. It is the origin and basis of the landscape pattern which we view today and a vigorous and viable farming community is the essential foundation of the nation's food supply.

19

The central attraction of the North York Moors lies in the **wide expanses of moorland** stretching for miles to the horizon and clothed with a purple hue in late August and September when the heather is in bloom. Some 40% of the Park is open moorland and provides the largest area of heather covered upland in England.

Few plants can survive on the acid soils of the moorland, and heather owes its dominance to its special adaption to the harsh physical conditions. **Heather** grows slowly on the nutrient-starved soils taking about 15 years to reach old age and a height of 3 to 4 feet. It is a dry tough wiry plant with tiny leaves barely 1/16 of an inch long. The moor comes into its own true colour in the late August and September flowering season. A mass of tiny purple flowers carpets the high moors (one estimate puts it at 3,000 million flowers to a square mile).

At first sight the panorama of heather moor gives an appearance of 'sameness'. A closer look reveals that the heather is not all the one colour and it is not all the one height — there is a mosaic with shades of black, grey, green and brown. This is the pattern that the farmers and gamekeepers establish by **burning the heather.** The burning programme plays an important part in the two features of economic life in the moors — sheep rearing and grouse management.

Every year between the 1st November and the following 31st March great plumes of smoke may be seen rising above the high moors. These are the months during which a landowner may burn the heather moor without a fire licence. This burning is referred to as **'controlled burning'** of

The Central Attraction

Above: The Scotch heather or 'ling' as it is called comes into bloom in late August and September.

Below: Heather is adapted to survive the cold, inhospitable conditions of the open moor.

the heather. The farmers and gamekeepers simply burn off patches of old straggly heather — the burnt areas being known locally as 'swiddens' or 'swizzens'. The burning is done at the time of year when the peat is damp and on a day when the wind direction will carry the fire towards a natural break such as a road, stream or a swidden burnt the previous year. Unlike accidental fires that get out of control, swiddening does not generate as great a heat and hence the roots of the heather and the peat are not destroyed. By periodically burning off the old woody heather, the roots are encouraged to produce **new green shoots** in the following years. It is these new shoots which provide a better feed for the sheep and grouse.

Uncontrolled moorland fires occur every year with disheartening repetition. There is no doubt about the cause of these fires — carelessness. **Carelessness** with a discarded match, cigarette end or picnic stove has meant fire and devastation to many areas of moor and forest. It is disastrous to stub out a cigarette end on dry heather or peat surface. The stub will 'catch' the peat and it may smoulder for hours until enough heat is generated to set the moor ablaze. Every now and again we enjoy a superb summer but when we do the **fire hazard** becomes extreme. In 1976, over 60 fires were recorded in various locations and in two instances the fire penetrated the deep peat causing it to burn for 3 months before the areas were declared 'safe'.

The message is clear to all of us, the greatest care must be taken to avoid destroying the very thing which we come to enjoy. If you see a fire — Dial 999, ask for FIRE and give as accurate a location as you can.

Sheep and Grouse

Sheep are an essential·part of the moorland scene. They are what the farmer calls **'heafed' to the moor** — each flock has a knowledge of its own particular stray or patch of moor which is acquired by each new generation. On the other hand, sheep do not have much road sense and some motorists drive far too fast on the unfenced moorland roads. The result is disaster, sheep and cars do not mix easily and in some cases up to 10% of the flocks, particularly the young lambs, are killed on the moorland roads each year.

It has been necessary to fence off the moorland along some stretches of the main roads through

the Park, but it is a costly exercise for the farmer and one which many people do not welcome in 'taming' the roadsides of the open moorlands. Part of the answer must be to **'drive carefully on country roads'**. Greater care, particularly at lambing time, is a small price to pay — both in respect of the farmer's livelihood and in avoiding injury or death to livestock.

The **red grouse** used to be called quite simply the 'moor bird'. Indeed, no other bird is quite so characteristic of and dependent upon the heather moorland. It appears a rather dark colour as it speeds over the moor in a low whirring flight and you will almost certainly hear its call of 'ge'bak, ge'bak' telling you to get back, get back! The grouse requires just one main source of food — heather, and in particular the young green shoots which are the most nutritious. However, they prefer old heather for **nesting cover** and therefore the gamekeeper tries to produce a mosaic of adjoining areas of young and old heather in order to support the maximum number of grouse. As we have already seen, the gamekeeper increases the food supply of young shoots by a programme of burning the moor.

The grouse population is of course kept artificially high for its sporting value. When the 12th August is announced as the **'glorious 12th'** it refers to the start of a new grouse shooting season. For four months (12th August-10th December) shooting parties appear on the moor as they have done for the last 100 years or so and you may see the beaters walking in line to raise the birds in the direction of the shooters. The **shooting butts** which screen the shooters, are an inescapable feature of the central moorlands. Most of them are soundly built of stone with a covering of heather so that they become part and parcel of the moorland landscape.

Opposite top left: The ownership of moorland sheep is established by a system of sheep markings which include paint marks, ear marks and horn marks.

Above: The red grouse is found only in heather moorland.

Opposite bottom right: Shooting butts are built in a line across various parts of the moorland.

From a Carriage Window

Below: Emerging from Grosmont Tunnel.
Opposite: At the northern end of Newton Dale.

Like a woodworker with his chisel, nature uses the tremendous power of moving water to carve out the network of valleys in the landscape. The very beautiful dale of **Newton Dale** was created just over 10,000 years ago towards the end of the period we call the Ice Age. To understand the making of this impressive dale you have to imagine millions of gallons of meltwater, from the moorland ice and snow, rushing southwards in the direction of Pickering. Within the space of maybe 10 or 20 years this huge channel had been created — a sort of miniature Grand Canyon.

As you motor along the Whitby road north out of Pickering you catch the occasional glimpse of this steep-sided valley. However, the real splendours of Newton Dale are reserved for those who view it either on foot or from a carriage window. It was 'the father of railways', **George Stephenson**, who appreciated the potential of Newton Dale as part of the route of his railway from Whitby to Pickering. The 26th May 1836 provided a great and colourful occasion in the histories of both Whitby and Pickering — it was the official opening of the railway. Within the space of 3 years, George Stephenson and his colleagues had completed some spectacular engineering feats in building a **24 mile railway line** through the heart of the North York Moors. For the first 11 years of its life it was less of a 'railway' and more of a 'tramway' on which passenger carriages and freight wagons were pulled along the route by **horse power**.

Charles Dickens travelled on this railway and commented on one of the most fascinating features of the original line where 'passengers are hauled by a rope'. He was referring to the 1 in 15 **Beck Hole incline**. The gradient was too steep for either horses or locomotives and a rope-

worked system was used to haul the carriages up to Goathland Bank Top Station. The incline was eventually abandoned in favour of the present route along the Eller Beck valley to Goathland.

After almost 130 years of railway traffic, the economics of the day directed that the Grosmont to Pickering section of the railway was to close on 8th March 1965. Another era had ended, another line had been **closed**. In spite of all the odds, a tiny band of railway enthusiasts had other ideas. They were convinced that with enough voluntary labour the line could be re-opened as a viable proposition. With the aid of grants from the Tourist Board and the National Park Committee, with efforts and enthusiasm too great to tell here, that 'dream' came true. The culmination was the official **re-opening ceremony** on Tuesday 1st May 1973 performed by the Duchess of Kent.

The rebirth of the line is a story of success. The railway now generates over 300,000 passenger journeys a year and has become the largest single tourist draw in the North York Moors. Apart from the opportunity to re-live the days of **steam**

railways you can view the engine repairs from the Grosmont loco shed gallery, visit the Information Centre at Pickering and explore the countryside along the waymarked walks from each of the stations. Forest walks can be explored from the Newtondale Halt deep inside the valley. The 'Historical Railway Trail' booklet describes the pleasant walk along the track-bed of the **original route** from Goathland down the Beck Hole incline and along the Murk Esk Valley to Grosmont.

British Rail also operates a rail service through the North York Moors — along the **Esk Valley Line** from Middlesbrough to Whitby. The railway provides a delightful scenic route, keeping close company with the River Esk on its way down to the sea. The station at Battersby Junction, five miles east of Stokesley, is worth seeking out. You can park your car here and start your railway journey down the Esk Valley. There are ten village stations along the line from which to enjoy many fine walks. From Danby Station there is a pleasant one mile walk to **The Moors Centre** where you will find more information available on **exploring the North York Moors**.

Trees in the Landscape

Trees are such an accepted part of our landscape that we tend to take them for granted. Only a few windswept conifers have managed, as seedlings, to escape the notice of the grazing sheep and to survive the conditions of the high moor. Forestry Commission plantations apart, it is in the dales and on the lower slopes of the Hambleton and Tabular Hills that we find a patchwork of fields, small woods, shelter belts and hedgerow trees.

Trees may either be self-sown from seed or planted by man. Only on the fenced-off steep slopes are the **natural woodlands** likely to regenerate and avoid the influence of man and beast. Many of our hedgerow trees are ash and sycamore as a result of their winged seeds being

Dalby Forest Drive

We tend to look upon the heather clad moors as the 'natural' vegetation, yet until the advent of Bronze Age Man (1800-500 B.C.) our upland tracts were clad with forest. Research into the moorland peat has revealed pollen from birch, hazel, pine, alder, oak, elm, willow, lime and yew — all components of the **prehistoric forest**. Our ancestors have succeeded in destroying the woodland cover; grazing sheep and heather burning now effectively prevent the growth of seedling trees. It is interesting to see that a scrub woodland of self-sown birch, hazel, pine etc. has established itself in the Bridestones Nature Reserve (north of Low Dalby). This woodland began to appear soon after the area had been fenced off from grazing sheep.

wind-borne. The seeds are caught in the hedgerows where they germinate. In a modern agricultual landscape there is little chance for self-sown trees to escape the blades of the hedge trimmer and there are often good agricultural reasons for taking out and not replacing hedgerow trees. Surveys regrettably show that a quarter of the Park's **hedgerow trees** could disappear within the next 10 to 15 years. Apart from their beauty, trees are necessary for our own existence (they complement our own requirements by taking in carbon dioxide and giving out oxygen to the air) and also play an essential part in the **wildlife food chain**.

An answer to the loss of trees is to take a **positive step** towards maintaining this feature of the landscape which we all enjoy. The Park Authority does this by providing farmers and landowners with trees which may be planted in rough, unproductive ground, awkward field corners and as replacements.

The **Forestry Commission** has reversed the trend of centuries and has been planting woodlands in the North York Moors since 1920 when land was first acquired north of Thornton Dale. The species of trees which the forester can grow are dictated by the physical conditions of soil and climate. It may be easier on the eye to view a woodland of mixed hardwoods but the first objective of the forester is to produce the nation's timber on an economic basis. Only the **coniferous trees** are hardy enough to produce an economic return on the impoverished soils and relatively inhospitable conditions of the moorland. Some 15% of the National Park is now covered with Forestry Commission coniferous plantations. Not only has a new dimension been added to the landscape but the forests have become a valuable **recreational resource**. The Forestry Commission has established a forest drive, a number of trails, a forest centre (Low Dalby), a camping and caravan site, forest cabin accommodation for visitors and the forests are generally open to walkers.

Robin Hood's Bay

A Coastal Excursion

The roads that reach down to the sea are few in number and virtually confined to those that lead to just a handful of villages. With so little human interference it is not surprising that our coastline rejoices in unspoilt splendour. The place where sea meets land has its own special air of **mystery and drama**. It is an area where some of the richest scenery can only be reached on foot and the coastal section of the **Cleveland Way** long distance footpath provides an excellent routeway along the cliff tops. Many stretches of unspoilt coastline in England and Wales have been defined by the Countryside Commission as 'Heritage Coasts' with the aim of promoting the conservation of the coastal scenery and encouraging informal recreational activities. This particular coastline has been defined as the 'North Yorkshire and Cleveland Heritage Coast' stretching beyond the National Park boundary from Saltburn-by-the-Sea to Scalby Ness, Scarborough.

The northern extremity of the Park boundary is at Boulby where the cliff towers 666 feet above sea-level and is the **highest point** on the east coast of England. Just 3 miles down the coast, Roxby Beck reaches the sea through a deep valley cut in the coastal rocks. The little inlet, bounded to the north by the striking cliff of Cowbar Nab, affords both shelter and sea access for the picturesque fishing village of **Staithes**. You can turn the clock back here a couple of centuries. Nothing has dramatically altered the character of the village since young **James Cook** was apprenticed to a local draper and grocer in the 1740s. However, the shop is no longer there — it was torn away in the 18th century by the raging sea which pounds this coastline. The Cod and Lobster Inn bravely faces the sea but 3 times it has been washed away and 3 times it has been rebuilt, the last occasion being in 1953.

During the early 19th century, Staithes was the most important fishing port on the whole of the Yorkshire coast. The traditional fishing craft was the **coble** (pronounced 'cobble' in Yorkshire). The design of the boat may be 1,000 years old dating back to the Vikings but it is still used today by the inshore fishermen of Staithes and Robin Hood's Bay.

Despite the lack of cobles, the village of **Runswick** retains its seafaring aspect. The village is in fact the second 'Runswick' for the original village, with the exception of just one cottage, slipped into the sea in 1682. A disaster fund was set up and the **village re-built.** The Jurassic shales which outcrop along the coast are relatively soft and slippery; once the base of the cliff has

Fishermen's boats at Staithes

been eroded by the sea a landslip is almost inevitable.

The village of **Robin Hood's Bay** has a romantic name and tales to match. Legend has it that the notorious outlaw of the greenwood forest sought refuge here from his pursuers. The isolation of the bay made an ideal landing spot for **smugglers** in the late 18th and early 19th centuries when virtually the whole village was involved in the trade of illicit goods. The village consists of the old part, locally called 'Bay Town' or just 'Bay' and the more recent development above. The headlands of North Cheek and South Cheek contain an impressive 3 mile sweep of the bay with the red-roofed village tightly packed at the northern end. The only main street leads you directly to the sea with a maze of dark alleyways giving access to the old houses. At low tide you can see the sweeping curves of hard rock ledges or **scars** reaching out into the bay. These scars are all that remain of a huge dome, centred in the middle of the bay, which has been eroded away in the geological past. The character and uniqueness of 'Bay' will live on, protected now by the 40 foot high sea wall completed in 1974.

At the extreme southern end of Robin Hood's Bay is the windswept village of **Ravenscar**, 600 feet above sea-level. The Romans took advantage of the headland view and built a look-out and signal station here. In the 18th century the site was used to build a substantial private residence, now the Raven Hall Hotel. If Ravenscar gives a feeling of 'emptiness' it is not altogether surprising. This is **'the town that never was'**. In the early 1900s ambitious plans were laid to build a seaside resort rivalling Whitby and Scarborough but the cliff-top site did not attract many buyers. The building company went bankrupt and the overgrown roads and building plots are all that remain of other men's dreams.

Wildlife

We have all become familiar enough with the word **'conservation'**. It appears in books, newpapers and television programmes and seems to cover just about everything in our environment — clean air, ancient buildings, glass bottles, whales, heating in our houses etc. In its widest sense, conservation is concerned with a **wise use of all our resources**, including wildlife. It will indeed be a wise course which ensures that our wildlife heritage is preserved alongside all the other interests in a National Park.

We do have some measure of **protection for wildlife** within what are known as Sites of Special Scientific Interest of which there are over 20 in the Park including one National Nature Reserve (Forge Valley), one Local Nature Reserve (Farndale) and eight Nature Reserves managed by the **Yorkshire Wildlife Trust.** You will need a permit from the Trust's offices at York to visit their Reserves as the Reserves are not always on public rights of way. **Farndale** was designated a Local Nature Reserve in 1955 to protect the colony of wild daffodils. Each spring time, nature spreads a yellow carpet along the banks of the River Dove and its tributaries. No one is allowed to pick the **wild daffodils,** ensuring that they are there for all to enjoy.

Any visitor to the North York Moors will soon appreciate the variety of scenery and wildlife habitats that exist in the Park — high cliff, rocky sea shore, sheltered woodland, coniferous forest, farmland, bog, riverside and windswept moor. This variety has in turn resulted in a wealth of wild flowers to be found in the Park and encouraged a wide range of birds into the area.

Above: The curlew is Britain's largest wader. It leaves the coast each spring to nest on the moor and upland farmland.

Opposite: Cross-leaved heath (large rose-pink flowers) and bell heather (deep purple) appear amongst a patch of ling. These are the three types of heather which grow on the moor.

An interest in wildlife starts for most of us with **identification** — the simple pleasure which is had from being able to put the right name to a bird, animal, flower or tree. Nevertheless, that knowledge does have to be acquired. We need to know where to look and what to look for. All the National Park Information Centres stock an interesting range of nature books which will help you start on your wildlife trail.

Two resident birds of **the moor** are the red grouse and meadow pipit. The lapwing, golden plover and curlew arrive in the spring to take up temporary residence in time to nest, lay, sit, hatch and raise their families. The **lapwing** is an easily spotted and distinctive bird on the moor. If you are close enough, you will see that its head is adorned with a long, black upturned crest. The moor is the home of the only **poisonous snake** that we have in Britain. It has a small flat head with dark zig-zag markings on a palish grey background. The **adder** is a timid, wary creature. It likes to bask in the sun but does not wait around for human inspection. Very rarely, people do get bitten by an adder; it is then necessary to keep the person at rest and to telephone the police for rescue and hospital treatment. The plant life of the open moor is of course dominated by heather. With a closer look you should be able to distinguish the three different types of heather. The dominant plant is Scotch heather or **ling** as it is called, which is in bloom from early August to late September. If you see patches of heather in flower during July then look for the difference between the deep purple flowers of the **bell heather** and the lighter pink flowers of the **cross-leaved heath**, the latter occupying the wetter sites.

It is in **the broadleaved woodlands** that we find the greatest variety of animal, bird and plant life. Much of the animal life of the woodland is nocturnal, but if you are around in the early morning or just before dusk you will get the best chance of seeing the fox, badger and rabbit. There are also red, roe and fallow deer in the woodlands of the Park. They are not easy animals to locate but at least their tracks can be observed along the forest rides on the damp mud or winter snow. The **roe deer** is the smallest of the three, being about 24 inches high at the shoulder. A fleeting glimpse may be all you have of this charming and agile creature for it is highly suspicious of strange sights and sounds. The **chaffinch** is perhaps the commonest bird in the wooded valleys and they have become quite tame in the car parks and picnic spots — quick to respond to crumbs of food offered by visitors. The flash of white on the shoulder, wing-bar and tail make it easily recognised. Close at hand you will be able to see the colourful plumage of the cock chaffinch with his slate-blue head, green rump and pinky-brown underparts. Woodlands and their edges provide a delightful range of wild flowers. All wild flowers require a certain amount of sunlight but carpets of **bluebells** and **wood anemones** can be found in quite dense woodland because they grow and flower in spring before the leaves of the trees blot out the sun.

The coastal belt is characterised by a line of steep, high cliffs but there are no areas of sand dunes or salt marshes. True maritime flowers are few in number but this is compensated for in the variety of common flowers which have established themselves in the areas of boulder clay, for example the **primrose**. Primroses thrive on clayey soil and they provide a beautiful array of colour along the cliffs in springtime. One true maritime flower to look for is **scurvy grass** with its flat-topped cluster of white flowers and rounded kidney shaped leaves. Its name gives a hint to its ancient use by sailors to provide vitamins in their

Above: A young roe deer
Top left: Daffodils in Farndale
Bottom left: A rare sight of an adder

diets and thereby avoid the disease of scurvy. The summer is a rewarding time to sit on the cliff tops and observe the sea-birds. The herring gull is the commonest of the larger gulls but far more enchanting is the **fulmar** with its silver-grey upperparts. It belongs to the Petrel family and at close range you will see the two short-tubed nostrils atached to its bill. The fulmar keeps its wings rigid as it soars and glides majestically along the air currents close to the cliff face.

33

A Precious Resource

Natural landscape beauty is a precious resource which deserves the concern of everyone who draws pleasure and inspiration from our countryside. The best of our landscapes form a national heritage which is protected for the enjoyment of all. The National Park Authority must follow the guidelines laid down in the 1949 Act of Parliament entitled 'National Parks and Access to the Countryside'. The 1949 Act clearly states that the duties are to **preserve the natural beauty** of the countryside, to **promote the enjoyment** of the public and to **pay due regard** to the interests of those who live and work in the Park.

These are very fine objectives. The next step is more difficult — the everyday business of answering the demands and desires of individuals, groups or organisations upon the countryside. We all place different and sometimes **conflicting demands** upon the National Park. It is a place to grow crops, rear livestock, plant trees, mine minerals, shoot grouse, walk over, drive through and build houses, car parks, caravan sites and reservoirs.

Ever since Bronze Age man began the first clearance of the natural forest, we have continued to expand our activities over the land. The present heather cover is maintained by a programme of periodic burning as a part of the management of the moor for sheep grazing and grouse conservation. This backcloth of heather is one that most people would not wish to see altered either to grass fields or coniferous forest — even if it was economically possible. However, over the last 30 years about 25% of open moorland has been ploughed out and used for agriculture and forestry. The demand for more food and more timber is still with us, so **what is the future** for the National Park? The National Park Authority, in trying to preserve this stretch of wild moorland, must therefore maintain close liaison with the farmers and foresters and must consider the payment of compensation or the purchase of land if necessary, to retain any area of outstanding landscape value.

The geology of our upland areas is such that they are the areas where important mineral resources are to be found. **Potash** for example is of such national importance as a source of agricultural fertilizer that planning permission was given in the North York Moors for its extraction at Boulby. However, an application for a second site was refused — the local, regional and national reasons for a second mining complex were not proved to override the loss in landscape value.

It is important that all applications for **new buildings** in the Park are considered against the impact on scenery and the village environment. Decisions must be made, for example, on the design of a new house in a village. To preserve the character of the village, the new property must 'fit in' with the rest of the village. It will generally be built in stone with a red clay pantile roof which are the traditional materials of the area.

Natural landscape beauty is the most **precious resource** which we have in the North York Moors. As time goes on, it is continually threatened by the pressure for development and recreation. How shall we judge the 'success' of our National Park in the context of conflicting demands? Our title page quotes some words of St. Ailred who was the third abbot of Rievaulx Abbey in the 12th century. He wrote that he found in these moors and dales 'peace, everywhere serenity

Above: The River Esk at Lealholm
Below: Great Fryup Dale

and a marvellous freedom from the tumult of the world'. Perhaps we can count success by the understanding and concern we show for these moors and in our efforts to ensure that the sentiments expressed by St. Ailred will remain. In the final analysis that is what our National Parks are all about — **peace, beauty and enjoyment.**

Information Centres

There is no substitute for the real thing — in this case, the countryside. The four walls of an exhibition room can never fully convey the experiences of being out in the countryside — the encouraging sense of spring as the primrose appears, the explosive flight of a disturbed grouse or that first glimpse of a beautiful view. The National Park Information Centres are there however, to introduce and interpret the countryside and hopefully, to **enhance our appreciation** of it. There is a bookshop in each centre with a wide range of books, maps and guides on the National Park and countryside interests.

The main visitor centre is **The Moors Centre** which has been adapted from a former shooting lodge. The centre aims to give you as full an introduction to the North York Moors as its facilities can provide and a visit here is an invaluable start to **exploring the North York Moors.** The centre provides a large exhibition area,

quiz trails, brass rubbing and pathfinder course. Tea Rooms provide refreshments and you can enjoy 13 acres of riverside, meadow, woodland, formal gardens and picnic areas. The centre is open daily between April and October and during February, March and November. School visits are welcomed provided they are booked in advance.

Sutton Bank Information Centre lies at one of the busiest main road entrances to the Park with some fine views from the top of Sutton Bank. There are displays on items of interest and places to visit in the south-west area of the Park. The Centre is open daily from Easter to 31st October and refreshments are available from the Refreshment Bar.

Pickering Station is the southern terminus of the North York Moors Railway where there are displays on the early history of the railway and a small audio-visual theatre. Refreshments are available and the Centre is open daily, all year.

Information Centres

The Moors Centre, Lodge Lane,
Danby, Whitby YO21 2NB.
Tel: Castleton (0287) 60654

Sutton Bank Information Centre, Sutton, Thirsk YO7 2EK.
Tel: Thirsk (0845) 597426

Pickering Station Information Centre, Pickering YO18 7AJ.
Tel: Pickering (0751) 73791

National Trust Information Centre, Ravenscar.
Tel: Scarborough (0723) 870138

Forest Visitor Centre, Low Dalby, Pickering.
Tel: Pickering (0751) 60295

Ryedale Folk Museum, Hutton-le-Hole.
Tel: Lastingham (07515) 367

The National Park Department publishes a range of leaflets, booklets and posters. Publication Lists and other information are available by post from the North York Moors National Park Department, The Old Vicarage, Bondgate, Helmsley, York YO6 5BP.

Guided Walk party at The Moors Centre